MW01166007

Nettles and Thistles

poems by

Hilda Weaver

Finishing Line Press
Georgetown, Kentucky

Nettles and Thistles

ACKNOWLEDGMENTS

The author wishes to thank the publishers of these previously printed poems:

"How to Uncover a Secret"   94 Creations, 4, 2013

"Maundy Thursday"   Offcourse, Issue 54, September 2013
"I Want Some *Times of Yesterday*"

"Emmanuel"   Licking River Review, Volume 43,
                                                      Winter 2011/Spring 2012

"The Gospel According to Elisabeth"   sugared water, 001,
                                                                Summer & Fall 2013

Publisher: Leah Maines
Editor: Christen Kincaid
Cover Art and Design: Carol Fountain Nix, www.carolfountainnix.com
Author Photo: Penelope Parsons, Raleigh, North Carolina

Printed in the USA on acid-free paper.
Order online: www.finishinglinepress.com
                also available on amazon.com

Author inquiries and mail orders:
Finishing Line Press
P. O. Box 1626
Georgetown, Kentucky 40324
U. S. A.

Table of Contents

They shall name it No Kingdom
There,
and all its princes shall be nothing.
Thorns shall grow over its
strongholds,
nettles and thistles in its fortresses,
an abode for ostriches.
Wildcats shall meet with hyenas,
goat-demons shall call to
each other;
there too Lilith shall repose,
and find a place to rest.

Isaiah 34:12-14 NRSV

*..for all the Liliths
who never found
a place to rest*

These Were the Women

These were the women, old, not old
enough, who dragged their homespun
skirts through dust, mud,
briars, on the tilted land
behind a sag-back mule.
Sharp toddler elbows,
number two or three,
pinched heavy, used up hips.
No soft imaginings or whisperings at night
to plan tomorrow's furrows,
only swift, perhaps not unkind sex.
Outside the smell of logs, whistlings
in Kentucky coffee bean, oak trees, and golden rod.
These were the women who came first, who died
on swept dirt floors exhausted in childbed,
hope gone from smiles too long ago to be
remembered. Mouths could not recite
the words of favorite hymns,
never spoke the number to be
multiplied, but knew to clamp
complaint. Drooped breasts and shoulders
greeted morning and day's end the same.
No matter this. They stayed behind the mules
and carried next year's babies in flaccid belly
sacks, the wonder oozed from eyes
which held no longer spark.

How to Uncover a Secret

No gold. But the *Zimbabwe* refugee, burned over his entire body, searches anyway, goes home to sticks piled up against *mumasa* not knowing of raped babies in the *Congo* and in *Somalia* no one cares if a cadaverous child, hair on end like a tiara decorated by biting flies, wheezes his last breath between cracked lips thick with his mother's matted spit like the mother in *Delhi* who has sold her girl child for the price of one small curry seed seeded offal of sacred cows which haven't yet unfurled their tongues to lick that tall slim man who wears a silk print Pierre Cardin tie.

Maundy Thursday

What if he could be a pole held up above
        a fishing pond
        thick ripped
        with artificial waves,
tsunamis in a scientific fix-it tank?

Or what if he could walk the sea
        to see you
        on the other side,
        a watered waif
held fast inside a plastic microchip?

Suppose his incarnation learned
        to sing
        in croaks and spits,
        curl tongued
the x's and the y's of plane geometry.

Suppose he dies beneath the Easter moon
        cracked cruel,
        to whisper wound
        the equinox.
Post his death on Facebook later on in May.

Emmanuel

She smells the cave gas grown explosive with the piss
and shit of mules and cows, shudders at the grime
of littered earth stomped down by rotted years of filth.
Squatting in the straw, pain in her gut, she pushes,
groans, calls out in hateful oath her husband's name, he
who put her in this foul and awful place. She's seized
by cramping fists, throws her hand into the spoor of goat,
curses at her pelvis open to night's air. She knows
her life will dwindle in excruciating bits, no-matterness
against the child who batters with a fury to be
gone from her. She doesn't want the others who have come
to sneer, vile as the place she has to drop this
nine-month requiem. Kings, angels, storied star she does not need,
not anyone, not even she impels this bloody birth.
When finally she gives in to it, gives up to it, he comes dumped damp
in spiked old grass, cord in his hand, last tie to her
too young to carry him. Drained from the carnage of her body's
weariness, wary of his squalling start, pain greater
than her labor was, she sees his genitals, a ragged slash along his side,
red tortured markings on his hands and feet.

God With Us Yesterday

In Memoriam
Matthew Shepard 1976—1998

So in your fury to be born,
God anointed you.
Give ground then, infant boy,
no matter that the mob spits filth
and crucifies you on a fence.

So be that man child then
not just another straggler though—
pass by us easily
while some, like God, may un-object,
remember how to love.

untitled color wrong

....the color is all wrong
....blue for sad
   why blue
   why not tangerine
....even skies cry
   tangerine
   before
   the night

Crown of Daisies

I was trying to find
my baptismal certificate

eighty-some odd years
too late, when I ran across

the picture that we liked,
the one of you turned slightly

toward my camera's lens,
woven daisies in your hair,

wry, almost seductive sneer
across the coral of your mouth.

Don't you remember that park
day? We were not naive

but we were younger then,
still absorbed the juices of our sex—

women in love, sunk in love,
mired in love, boxed by "no"

but there it was, the hormone flash,
excitement marked, as chiggers

bit coronas on your head
and mine. It was a sign we didn't read.

Picnic

Why don't we take a picnic
to the high spot
way above the river's snake
meanderings?
We can build a fire
with our small briquettes,
roast hot dogs there,
drink wine,
bat off mosquitoes
as the dusk drives in.
Then we can sit
uncomfortably,
two women holding hands,
ponder about us and watch
some children on the swings.

Patterned Light

Morning did not break today
but came with slithering ease,
breaking up the night
as if it were a too old,
not remembered toy.

In its brokenness were pulses
of the day to come
where not one pattern
would remain the same.

As strips of fractured light
shift across this writing page,
I remember you
the way you skipped across my life.

The Gospel According to Elisabeth

(Elisabeth Kubler-Ross, *On Death and Dying; the five stages of grief*)

I need to talk with you.
I see the kiln red marker
in the ground
—your name.
I hope you
won't be late tonight.

I stand on my head, do cartwheels in the sand of future oceans we
will cross, crisscross across the flex of yesterday's abundance, call
you to come, come up, come away, come on. You won't surrender
your identity to join the fantasy of places not yet visited, hitch a
trailer to the car or to the stars for all I care, just come with me. I
ask God to take away your disappear; She doesn't answer me.

You in the emergency room
under sterile sheets again.
Back at the B & B
I chew my lip and watch
the fallow deer.
I've lost the siren's pitch.
Go, damn you,
goddamn you
anyway.

When I'm through, I'm done, I'm gone.
All the *gones*, like day old Krispy Kremes—rotten holes and all.
More and more my head precedes my shoulders when I walk the
dog.

You're gone
frail as the Spanish moss
above your head.
Soon enough my ashes
will be boxed up
next to yours.

Question of Mismatch

The irises I cut
stood up
too tall
for that old vase
which didn't match
them anyway.
What do you call it
when the flower clashes
with its urn?
We have to call
it something,
don't we?
When we sat down
beside each other
in the long oak pew,
we didn't call it anything.

Where I Haven't Been

Nothing in my life has been about tomorrow's hope,
yet I have lived with it, lived in it,
lived excuses for decisions based on it,
resisted love and chased it, till my breath ran out.
It ran out long ago, carried by a nuthatch
in the corner of the self I turned around to see.

Color Me Us

It all comes back to us,
doesn't it? Poet, do you not marvel
at astounding red, woodpecker cap,
rose thorn, earlier than Spring
the tulip rising through the snow?
Do you not notice purple,
gray blue, teal, umber
in the mountain's rise, sun up,
sun down against the scarlet scab?
Are not living things like chipmunks
striped in readiness to scoot away?
Why can't these suffice?
Why is it always about us?

Bus Ride with an Intimate Stranger

One day I asked a tanager
to sit beside me
on the bus; his color
filled the bench. He was careful
not to bend his feathers
on the plastic seat.
We rode together for a good
long time, many years
in fact. He wanted to be
gone, but he was imprisoned
there, held fast
by my fixed gaze, afraid
to move. Instead, he bonded
with the bus.
Several folks got off
and on, remarked
about the palette
of his plumage, remarked
he was a quiet bird
for all his rich display.
The bus just kept a bounce,
prickly in each season's tide.
As we rode, we moved
into ravines,
and all the while
he didn't move a bite away
from me.

Five Lived Years

Your fingers twitch
to please yourself.
Alone with me, you think
you have the right.
You do—you have the right.
I am only sickly five
under covers in my bed,
five lived years beneath
your thirtysome.

Portrait of Lakshmi

When I see the photo of the old woman
whose husband deliberately ate pesticide,
I can count the cross hatched lines,
furrowed, like rows of soy beans
across her face, even on her lips,
her chin. A single dot
between her eyebrows seems to weep
the oil of cataracts into her rheumy eyes,
desolate below the pewter hair
and dirty scarf. Rarely have I seen a face
more beautiful, more familiar
with catastrophe. I want to trace a gentle lip
balm smooth across her mouth,
ease my little finger down the lines
below her cheeks, feel her skin
patina-ed as fine leather is. A small bead
pierces through her long, straight nose.
Her face speaks pinched, relentless poverty,
and loss of him who gave her nothing
while he lived, nothing when he died.

Raven's Tongue

The second was a girl child too,
dark haired, unlike the first
whose hair was almost white.
My mother would refuse to wash
their names in Tide
with foamy chlorine bleach.
They were called too much alike.
Two little girls who could not ask
a prim-lipped Gran
to hold their hands
or tickle the sweet breath
breathed fresh, popsicle lipped.
She missed round buttocks
in her hands; she never learned
to spare a hug for them—or me.
Once I saw her watching them
as closely as a raven might consider
his first meal. She shook her head
and turned away. She had no appetite
for anything that wasn't male.

I Want *Some* Times of Yesterday

I want to hide among the roots
  eroded, bare along the creek,
and be like beetles pushing dung
  or ants which carry burdens
bigger than themselves.

I want to hear sharp splashes
  like the acorns make before squirrels
notice they are gone, or watch
  the moccasin uncurl, expose
its younglings to the sun.

I want to jump and grab the grapevine
  just beyond my reach and swing
across the creek, make it to the other side,
  and feel the mushy sand creep
sideways through my toes.

I want to catch a chortling frog
  to hold until I hear the dinner bell,
until I'm called back home
  to rhubarb pie, sweet corn, churned cream,
kittens on the porch.

OK to Laugh

Yesterday I looked at old photo albums
as if by chance and not.

We looked so happy in those pictures.
We could laugh at too tight sweaters,

silly postures,
hairstyles straight from hell's salon,

figurines that cluttered
up the shelves.

It didn't matter much.
I just hate to be reminded

it was OK
to laugh back then.

Two Days Before Tomorrow

I want to commune
with adolescent
chimpanzees
or toddler giraffes.
This is the day
when communion
takes the form of apple
cider steeped in virginal
displays.
No orangutan feels
sorry for itself.
This is the day
when even cockatoos
make love.

Lilith

"...there too Lilith shall repose,
and find a place of rest."   Isaiah 34:14 (NRSV)

I'll find a place of rest,
not as a mile marked traveler sleeps,
but like a butterfly,
stigmata stippled on its wings,
wounded on the journey south
to temperatures of tolerated warmth,
or like a parson paused to rest his voice,
or like a woman who's forgotten
candied Christmases.

HILDA is a retired Marriage and Family Therapist and Addictions Counselor. After moving to Kentucky in 2010, she took courses at NKU, refining a lifetime's "dabbling" in the possibilities of poetry. "It takes many years," she says, "to hear your own voice". Her work has appeared previously in *94 Creations, Sugared Water, Licking River Review, Emily, Offcourse, Pidgeonholes, Uppagus,* and in a micro chapbook from Porkbelly Press entitled *The Autobiography of a Love Not Mine.* She is also one of four women (*wild soft*) whose collaborative poems have been published by several journals, including *Dancing Girl Press* and *Hermeneutic Chaos Press.*